AN

INNISFREE

A One Act Play
by

Jean Lenox Toddie

SAMUEL FRENCH, INC.
45 WEST 25TH STREET   NEW YORK 10010
7623 SUNSET BOULEVARD HOLLYWOOD 90046
LONDON   TORONTO

ISBN 0 573 62620 0   Printed in U.S.A.   # 3579

IMPORTANT BILLING AND CREDIT REQUIREMENTS

All producers of AND GO TO INNISFREE *must* give credit to the Author of the Play in all programs distributed in connection with performances of the Play and in all instances in which the title of the Play appears for purposes of advertising, publicizing or otherwise exploiting the Play and/or a production. The name of the Author *must* also appear on a separate line, on which no other name appears, immediately following the title, and *must* appear in size of type not less than fifty percent the size of the title type.

"I will arise and go now, and go to Innisfree,
And a small cabin build there, of clay and wattles made.
Nine bean rows will I have there, a hive for the honey bee,
And live alone in the bee-loud glade."

William Butler Yeats

CHARACTERS

OLD ANNA:
An older woman.

YOUNG ANNA:
The voice of her youth.

ANNA:
The voice of her middle years.

SCENE

A beach on the coast of New England.

TIME

September.

NOTES ON THE PLAY

As indicated in the costume plot, the three characters are similarly dressed. Interaction between the three women appears natural except for the fact that OLD ANNA never actually looks at the younger women, nor do they actually touch her.

If a director wishes to experiment, the movement of the younger women might be stylized, helping to establish them as inner voices, as well as adding to the pictorial quality of the production.

The title of the song sung by the three characters is "When You And I Were Young, Maggie," with music by J.A. Butterfield and words by George W. Johnson. It can be found in most collections of old songs popular in the earlier years of the century.

(SCENE: The stage is lit with soft pink light melting into lavender shadow. It is bare except for a single white stool stage center.)

(AT RISE: OLD ANNA enters stage left carrying a parasol flowered in shades of pink and rose. Moving down stage she looks out over the water.)

OLD ANNA: Suppose I were to take off my slippers and walk into the water, feel myself lifted and drawn out. Would there be time to think? Would I find myself thinking, "Oh, how I do love bacon sandwiches?"

ANNA: *(From the shadows up right)* Certainly not. *(Stepping from the shadows)* You would take a great gulp of sea water and think, "What a foolish old woman I am."

OLD ANNA: *(Laughs lightly)* Yes, I suppose I would.

YOUNG ANNA: *(Stepping from the shadows up left)* But, oh, how I ... *(Flinging her arms wide)* How I do love bacon sandwiches!

OLD ANNA: Crispy brown bacon ...

YOUNG ANNA: *(Skipping down to OLD ANNA)* On squishy white bread! *(Whispers in OLD ANNA's ear)* With oodles and oodles of butter!

OLD ANNA: Yes, oh, yes!

ANNA: *(Dryly)* Lovely for your cholesterol.

YOUNG ANNA: *(Twirling)* Lovely!

OLD ANNA: *(Lifts her shirt and twirls)* Lovely! *(Laughing, she stops twirling, closes her eyes and breathes deeply)* How I do love the scent of seaweed, the scent of seaweed and the sound of the surf.

ALL THREE: *(Breathe deeply)* Ahh ...

OLD ANNA: *(Opening her eyes she strolls stage left, turns and looks up the beach)* And here I am, standing on this barren beach in late September as I've done for the past fifty years. Skinny dipping with Daniel those first few years ...

ANNA: Sunburned and breathless.

OLD ANNA: Later with the children and then the grandchildren ...

YOUNG ANNA: *(Twirling stage left)* Pails, and shovels, and castles and kites!

OLD ANNA: And these last few years standing here alone.

ANNA & YOUNG ANNA: *(A soft echo)* Alone.

OLD ANNA: And now, old woman ... *(Lowers the parasol)* Where do you suppose you'll find yourself next September?

ANNA: To sell your house, what foolishness.

YOUNG ANNA: No!

OLD ANNA: No, it was time! Surely it was time. The bedrooms are empty now and the kitchen is quiet. The children come less often, they have so much to do. I, on the other hand, seem to have so little.

ANNA: *(Primly)* One must keep busy.

OLD ANNA: And I used to be so busy.

YOUNG ANNA: *(Twirling stage center)* One must ... *(She grasps OLD ANNA's hands and twirls her. Aside from the fact their hands do not quite touch, the action is realistic)* One must have fun!

OLD ANNA: *(Stops twirling, breathless)* Oh!

ANNA: Steady!
YOUNG ANNA: Steady!

*(ANNA and YOUNG ANNA guide OLD ANNA to the stool.
Again they do not actually touch her.)*

OLD ANNA: Steady you foolish old woman. *(Lowers
herself to the stool, closes her eyes, sits quietly a moment)*
What have I done? Oh, dear, what have I gone and done?

ANNA: *(Softly)* To sell your house, what foolishness.

YOUNG ANNA: *(Softly)* To sell your house, what fun.

OLD ANNA: *(Rubbing her temples)* My head goes ...

ANNA: *(Softly)* What foolishness.

YOUNG ANNA: *(Softly)* What fun.

OLD ANNA: ... Goes round and round ... *(Opens her
eyes)* And look at me sitting here talking to myself. If anyone
were to see me.

ANNA: *(Softly)* Foolishness!

OLD ANNA: Hush!

YOUNG ANNA: *(Softly)* What fun!

OLD ANNA: Why is it I can't make up my mind? When
I was younger I knew exactly what to do. I washed my
daughter's hair in rain water, soaked my husband's
handkerchiefs in lemon juice and cooked the oatmeal on the
range overnight as my mother used to do. And when I was a
little girl, well, there was just no stopping me.

YOUNG ANNA: *(Skipping stage right)* I could blow a
bubble that covered half my face!

ANNA: *(Crying out as a little boy would do)* Show-off!

(OLD ANNA laughs.)

YOUNG ANNA: And turn more cartwheels in the school yard than any other girl.

OLD ANNA: Even Elaine Bernhart, and she was in the fifth grade.

(YOUNG ANNA turns a cartwheel.)

ANNA: *(Again crying out)* We can see your panties!

YOUNG ANNA: *(Spins around and raises a fist)* Take that back!

OLD ANNA: *(Rising, she lifts a fist)* Take that back or I'll ...

YOUNG ANNA: Or I'll ...

OLD ANNA: *(Lowers her fist, laughs)* Look at me, standing here among these ... *(Mimes nudging something with her toe)* ... these rotting lobster pots as if I hadn't a care in the world when there's so much to do. Now what was it I was planning to do?

ANNA: *(Primly)* Make a list if you wish to remember.

OLD ANNA: If I wish to remember I must make a list. Let me see, did I ...

(Counts on her fingers as ANNA checks off items, and YOUNG ANNA responds.)

ANNA: Did I turn off the oven?

YOUNG ANNA: *(Twirling stage right)* Yes!

ANNA: Unplug the iron?

YOUNG ANNA: *(Twirling stage left)* Yes!

ANNA: Remember to carry my keys?

YOUNG ANNA: Yes, yes ...

OLD ANNA: Yes. The oven is off, the iron is unplugged, *(Mimes drawing keys from her skirt pocket)* and see, I've remembered to carry my keys! But ... but I'm sure there was something else. *(YOUNG ANNA runs to her and whispers in her ear)* Oh, my! *(Laughs)* How could I forget?

YOUNG ANNA: Forget the party!

OLD ANNA: My birthday party!

ANNA: Have you forgotten you invited the entire village?

OLD ANNA: Everyone?

YOUNG ANNA: Everyone!

ANNA: Every adult.

YOUNG ANNA: And every child!

OLD ANNA: Oh, my goodness, are the presents wrapped?

YOUNG ANNA: The presents are wrapped!

OLD ANNA: *(Moving stage left)* Mama's silver tea strainer and Aunt Addie's crystal bowl?

YOUNG ANNA: Yes!

OLD ANNA: There must be presents for the children, of course, children expect presents.

YOUNG ANNA: Teddy bears and balloons!

ANNA: But to give away grandmother's embroidered ...

OLD ANNA: Grandmother's embroidered pillow slips.

ANNA: The villagers will talk, you know.

OLD ANNA: Oh, dear.

ANNA: They'll gather in Taylor's Apothecary and tell each other you're mad.

OLD ANNA: Perhaps I am.

YOUNG ANNA: Who cares?

(Sticks out her tongue at ANNA.)

ANNA: And what will our letter carrier do with a cut glass salt dish?

YOUNG ANNA: Our letter carrier will love it!

OLD ANNA: And Emma Gaul ...

ANNA: Will Emma Gaul love the silver pickle fork?

OLD ANNA: Will she have use of it as she sets the table for a hungry husband just in from the sea ...

ANNA: And four children under six years of age?

YOUNG ANNA: She'll love it!

OLD ANNA: *(Sweeping stage right)* And as I'm selling the house I'll have no room for such things.

ANNA: No room for a silver pickle fork?

OLD ANNA: No room! I'm weary of polishing a pickle fork that's seldom put to use!

ANNA: Have you something better to do with your time?

OLD ANNA: There must be something better to do.

ANNA: Such as?

OLD ANNA: Yes?

OLD ANNA: I shall ...

ANNA: Yes?

YOUNG ANNA: *(Strutting stage right)* I shall go to the circus!

ANNA: What foolishness.

YOUNG ANNA: I shall go to the fair!

OLD ANNA: What fun!

ANNA: What nonsense.

(A moment's silence.)

OLD ANNA: Yes, what nonsense. You've sold your house, old woman, and now ...

ANNA: And now you had best listen to the children and rent a condominium in the retirement village down the road.

OLD ANNA: The children will insist.

YOUNG ANNA: *(Runs to OLD ANNA, whispers in her ear)* Phooey on the children!

OLD ANNA: Phooey. But I suppose it's ...

ANNA: It's the practical thing to do.

OLD ANNA: Yes.

ANNA: At your age.

OLD ANNA: At my age. But it's certainly not ...

YOUNG ANNA: Now what I want to do!

ANNA: What is it you want to do?

OLD ANNA: I want ...

ANNA: Yes?

OLD ANNA: I want to ...

YOUNG ANNA: I want to roller skate and ride my two-wheeler!

ANNA: And fall and skin your knees?

OLD ANNA: Yes.

YOUNG ANNA: I want to sit in the brambles again and eat blackberries!

OLD ANNA: And let the juice roll down my chin.

ANNA: And stain your midi-blouse, of course.

OLD ANNA: Of course.

YOUNG ANNA: And early in the morning before the sun is up I want to sneak downstairs when I hear the milkman.

OLD ANNA: And lick cream from the top of the bottle.

ANNA: Shame on you.

YOUNG ANNA: I want to climb to the top of the sliding

board, and jump off and find I can float! *(As she starts to twirl, OLD ANNA slowly twirls)* Look at me ...

OLD ANNA: I'm floating!

ANNA: *(Grasping YOUNG ANNA)* How long do you imagine you'll remain in the air, you wrinkled old balloon?

OLD ANNA: *(Opening her eyes, sighs)* You're not seventeen, you're seventy ...

ANNA: And when you land you'd best have a stove on which to set your kettle, for the only thing you'll want is ...

OLD ANNA: Is a good hot cup of tea.

YOUNG ANNA: No!

OLD ANNA: No.

YOUNG ANNA: *(Wrenches loose, runs stage left, drops to the floor, sits cross-legged)* I shall drink warm beer ...

OLD ANNA: And eat hard pretzels.

ANNA: Try to be serious.

OLD ANNA: But I am serious. That's what worries me. I have such odd thoughts of late. Sometimes when I close my eyes ... *(Closes her eyes)* I seem to see white cotton underwear bleaching in the sun.

ANNA: Now, now.

(Leads OLD ANNA stage center and lowers her to the stool.)

OLD ANNA: Why do you have such strange thoughts, old woman?

ANNA: Because you're worn out. You haven't been sleeping well lately, nor have you been eating properly.

OLD ANNA: Tea and toast is not proper nourishment.

ANNA: When you've moved into the condominium you'll find you sleep better and eat better. The meals are tasty and nutritious and there's a whirlpool bath.

YOUNG ANNA: I'd rather wash in rain water!

ANNA: *(Ignoring YOUNG ANNA)* The women you met seem congenial.

OLD ANNA: Wash in a barrel that's been sitting in the sun.

ANNA: There's maid service.

YOUNG ANNA: *(Jumping up)* Soak in the barrel when the water is warm!

ANNA: There are well tended gardens.

YOUNG ANNA: *(Spinning)* And lie naked in the weeds ...

OLD ANNA: While I dry.

ANNA: With the help of the children you'll be settled in the twinkling of an eye in a well tended condominium complex where you'll make friends with well-traveled women who ...

OLD ANNA: Who turn over your pickle fork to check that it's sterling and peek at the label in your coat!

ANNA: *(To OLD ANNA)* You think that because you're frightened of women in well-tailored suits. You haven't bought yourself a decent suit in years. Be honest, didn't the women you met look as if they would enjoy a good book, a good meal, good conversation?

OLD ANNA: And I suppose that does sound better than eating alone with no one to talk to but yourself.

ANNA: The children are right. You insisted on selling your house, now a retirement community is the proper place to be.

OLD ANNA: Yes, I suppose it is, but ...

YOUNG ANNA: But I'd rather study ants!

ANNA: Study ants?

OLD ANNA: What an odd thought. I have such odd thoughts of late.

YOUNG ANNA: *(Runs to OLD ANNA)* Remember the summer mama was away? Away nursing nana? You spent the days with Auntie Kate.

OLD ANNA: I haven't thought of Auntie Kate in years. Fancy I should remember.

YOUNG ANNA: She let you help with most everything, smoothing the sheets.

OLD ANNA: Plumping the pillows.

YOUNG ANNA: Rolling out the dough for the blueberry tarts.

ANNA: And handing her the clothes pins as she hung the laundry on the line.

(All three close their eyes, remembering that golden summer.)

OLD ANNA: *(Breathes softly)* Yes.
YOUNG ANNA & ANNA: *(Simultaneously)* Yes.

(A moment's silence.)

OLD ANNA: *(Suddenly)* White cotton underwear!

(Their eyes pop open.)

YOUNG ANNA & ANNA: *(Simultaneously)* White cotton underwear ...

OLD ANNA: Bleaching in the sun!

(They laugh.)

YOUNG ANNA: And when Auntie Kate rested after tea and tarts ...

OLD ANNA: I'd lie on my tummy in the garden and watch the bumble bees suck honeysuckle and the black ants scurry about ...

YOUNG ANNA: Under the blueberry bush!

OLD ANNA: *(Laughs)* Now let me see, how many legs does a black ant have?

ANNA: Six.

OLD ANNA: Yes, six legs! *(YOUNG ANNA mimes picking up an ant and counting its legs)* Such fun!

ANNA: *(Softly, in OLD ANNA's ear)* They'll whisper in Taylor's Apothecary, you know, they tell each other you're mad.

OLD ANNA: Perhaps they do. But how many of them know that an ant has six legs? *(Rises, raises the parasol, twirls it gaily as she moves stage left, followed by YOUNG ANNA, who mimes her movements)* What if I were to find myself a cottage where I could hang my underwear on the line to dry, and plant a blueberry bush and after tea and tarts stretch out on my tummy ...

YOUNG ANNA: And study ants!

OLD ANNA: *(Turns and strolls stage right)* Yes, why not? I could read about ants, learn everything there is to know about ants, become passionate about ant life. And in time some wayward child would stumble upon my cottage and run home to tell of the old lady who lives in the woods and talks to ants.

YOUNG ANNA: Yes!

OLD ANNA: And when the first reporter arrives to interview me I shall shoo him away with a broom, and ...

YOUNG ANNA: And rumors will fly!

OLD ANNA: Men of science will peep at me from behind bushes, and because they wear their hair long and don't clean their eye glasses I shall ask them in and demonstrate how I've taught my ants to ...

OLD ANNA & YOUNG ANNA: To dance!

(OLD ANNA drops the parasol. She and YOUNG ANNA do a
     little dance step. Laughing, OLD ANNA stops and wipes
     her forehead.)

ANNA: You had best stop that, you foolish old woman. Look at you, you're flushed. *(OLD ANNA picks up the parasol)* And you're not supposed to sit in the sun.

OLD ANNA: *(Returning to the stool)* And I'm not supposed to ...

YOUNG ANNA: Not supposed to roller skate!

ANNA: Roller skating at your age!

OLD ANNA: And not supposed to color my hair.

YOUNG ANNA: To color my hair green on St. Patrick's Day!

OLD ANNA: And I mustn't eat spicy food ...

YOUNG ANNA: When I love spicy food!

OLD ANNA: Chili and hot dogs.

YOUNG ANNA: Hot dogs with mustard!

OLD ANNA: And onions.

YOUNG ANNA: *(Dancing down to the water's edge)* And gobs and gobs of relish!

ANNA: *(To OLD ANNA)* The doctor told you ...

YOUNG ANNA: *(Mimes splashing her feet in the water)* Phooey on the doctor!

ANNA: *(To YOUNG ANNA)* Don't be an ass. *(Turns to OLD ANNA)* You'll grow accustomed to a condominium. No lawn to cut in summer, no drive to plow in the winter.

OLD ANNA: And the ladies say they haven't a moment to themselves, what with the book club and the bridge club. And I do enjoy a good book.

ANNA: And there's a painting class.

OLD ANNA: Do you suppose I could ...

ANNA: Of course you could. And don't forget the trips, trips to museums, concerts, plays. And there's a nine hole golf course.

OLD ANNA: Do you suppose I could ...

YOUNG ANNA: Phooey on golf! *(Mimes climbing a ladder)* I'd rather climb to the top of the sliding board and ... *(Mimes jumping off into the air)* ... jump!

ANNA: In a retirement home there would be someone around if you took a fall, or became ill in the wee hours of the night.

OLD ANNA: I shouldn't like to become ill in the wee hours of the night.

ANNA: And the retirement home is a block from the ocean. One could walk to the beach at night and watch the Pleiades dancing in silver surf.

YOUNG ANNA: On the hills back home moonlight silvers the tops of the pines and spills like honey over the mountain laurel.

OLD ANNA: *(Softly)* The hills of home.

ANNA: This is your home. Here where the sand smells of salt and the waves curve into lavender this time of day. It's been your home for fifty years. If you leave now you'll miss it terribly. And if you go through with this mad idea of giving away everything you own you'll find you miss mama's silver tea strainer and Aunt Addie's crystal bowl as well.

OLD ANNA: No, I'm weary of dusting and scrubbing and polishing.

YOUNG ANNA: *(Running to her)* You want to go barefoot and wiggle your toes, you want to take off your corset and wear a white robe!

ANNA: Why would you want to wear a white robe?

OLD ANNA: There was a reason, but ...

ANNA: But?

OLD ANNA: But it's slipped my mind. The villagers are right, I'm quite mad. *(Weeps soundlessly a moment, then straightens her back and lifts her chin)* Nonsense.

ANNA: Nonsense, you're overtired. All you need to do is sit down and sign the application for a condominium. It's the wisest thing to do. And what a relief to the children.

OLD ANNA: What a relief.

YOUNG ANNA: *(Drops to the sand beside OLD ANNA)* Let's go home.

ANNA: None of that.

YOUNG ANNA: I want to go home.

ANNA: Stop it.

YOUNG ANNA: I want to take Jiggs for a walk.

ANNA: Stop it this minute!

OLD ANNA: Jiggs?

ANNA: *(To OLD ANNA)* Shhh. *(Moves behind OLD ANNA, mimes gently rocking her)* You had a dog and you called him Jiggs, but that was long ago.

YOUNG ANNA: Back home?

(Although it is YOUNG ANNA speaking, ANNA's responses are now directed to OLD ANNA.)

ANNA: Yes.

YOUNG ANNA: Back home in the hills?

ANNA: That's right.

YOUNG ANNA: The hills of Pennsylvania?

ANNA: Your little fox terrier, remember?

YOUNG ANNA: Yes.

ANNA: But that was long ago. *(Moves down stage to look out over the water)* There's going to be a storm. *(Breathes deeply. As she does OLD ANNA and YOUNG ANNA also take a deep breath)* I can smell it.

YOUNG ANNA: Papa could smell a storm. He could smell the electricity in the air.

ANNA: He would walk out on the porch and take a deep breath. "There's going to be a storm ..."

YOUNG ANNA: He'd say.

ANNA: "And it's going to be a hum-dinger."

(All three smile, remembering papa.)

YOUNG ANNA: I miss my papa. *(ANNA nods)* Miss sitting on the porch with papa.

ANNA: On the swing.

YOUNG ANNA: Swinging.

ANNA: Jiggs chasing fireflies.

YOUNG ANNA: Mama at the window.

ANNA: Papa singing to her as the light fades.

OLD ANNA: *(Softly sings the words of an old song)* "I wander'd today to the hill, Maggie."

(Brief silence.)

YOUNG ANNA: Papa was the most popular man in town!

OLD ANNA: Indeed he was.

ANNA: Men walking down the alley ...

YOUNG ANNA: Down the alley of an evening ...

ANNA: Would holler, "Hey, Daniel!"

OLD ANNA: "Hey, Daniel, they would holler."

ANNA & YOUNG ANNA: *(Grasp hands and spin as they call)* Hey, Daniel!

ANNA: *(Stops spinning, embraces YOUNG ANNA, says softly)* But papa is gone.

OLD ANNA: Gone?

(Both turn to look at OLD ANNA.)

ANNA: Yes.

OLD ANNA: But I can see him sitting on the swing.

ANNA: You're overtired.

OLD ANNA: See him clear as day, swinging.

ANNA: Hush now.

OLD ANNA: Taking a deep breath ...

ANNA: Hush

OLD ANNA: Smelling the electricity.

ANNA: Shh.

OLD ANNA: The electricity in the air.

ANNA: Shh.

YOUNG ANNA: And Jiggs is whirling!

ANNA: Hush now.

YOUNG ANNA: *(Whirls across the stage)* Whirling!

ANNA: Hush.

YOUNG ANNA: *(Spinning wildly)* Whirling ... whirling!

OLD ANNA: *(Stumbles to her feet and cries out)* There's going to be a storm! *(All three stand motionless.) (Sinks down on the stool and whispers)* Oh, papa, there's going to be a storm.

(ANNA and YOUNG ANNA look at OLD ANNA with consternation.)

ANNA: *(To YOUNG ANNA)* Now see what you've done! *(To OLD ANNA)* If you behave like this no retirement home will have you.
OLD ANNA: Good!

(YOUNG ANNA runs stage left, mimes picking up a stone and throwing it at ANNA, who ducks. They glare at each other, fold their arms across their chests and simultaneously turn to stare out over the water. After a moment ANNA's face softens and she begins to sing.)

ANNA:
"I wander'd today to the hill, Maggie,
To watch the scene below;"
YOUNG ANNA: *(Her face softens. She joins in)*
"The creek and the creaking old mill, Maggie,
As we used to, long ago."
OLD ANNA: *(Sings the next two lines alone, her voice soft and sad)*
"The green grove is gone from the hill, Maggie,
Where first the daisies sprung;"
YOUNG ANNA: *(Turning, sees the sadness on OLD ANNA's face and picks up the tempo)*

"The creaking old mill is still, Maggie,
Since you and I were young."
*(ANNA claps and OLD ANNA taps her foot as YOUNG ANNA
repeats the final lines, dancing a little jig.)*
"The creaking old mill is still, Maggie,
Since you and I were young."

(All three laugh.)

> OLD ANNA: *(Gasps)* Oh!
> ANNA: What?
> YOUNG ANNA: What is it?
> OLD ANNA: There was an old mill.
> ANNA: An old mill?
> OLD ANNA: Down by Potter's stream.
> YOUNG ANNA: And a ...
> OLD ANNA: And a cottage.
> ANNA: Are you sure?
> YOUNG ANNA: Yes!
> OLD ANNA: Isn't that remarkable.
> ANNA: Remarkable?

OLD ANNA: I do believe it's the cottage I see in my dreams, a cottage curtained with cobwebs shining in the morning light.

YOUNG ANNA: With a tangle of wild honeysuckle, sweet and warm in the noonday heat!

ANNA: *(To YOUNG ANNA)* A tangle of yellow roses. *(To OLD ANNA)* Your memory is faulty, it's a sign of senility.

YOUNG ANNA: It's a privilege of age!

ANNA: One doesn't live alone when one's memory is faulty.

OLD ANNA: But if I were to buy that cottage I would wake to the high, clear call of the thrush and sit at the window and drink black coffee while I watched the sun come up.

YOUNG ANNA: As Mama sat at the window each evening.

ANNA: With lamplight in her hair.

YOUNG ANNA: *(Dropping to her knees beside OLD ANNA)* You were happy at home in the hills.

OLD ANNA: Yes.

ANNA: You've been happy here by the sea.

OLD ANNA: Yes.

(Confused, lifts a finger and nibbles a nail.)

ANNA: *(Smacks the offending hand)* Biting your nails at your age! Just look at your hands!

OLD ANNA: *(Studies her hands)* Just look at them.

YOUNG ANNA: *(Rocks back and hugs her knees)* "If a woman sits in the shade when she shells her peas ..."

ANNA: "Her skin will stay comely and white ..."

YOUNG ANNA: Mama said.

OLD ANNA: And here I am, wrinkled by the sun and weathered by the wind.

YOUNG ANNA: *(Giggles)* And your hair!

OLD ANNA: Papa said my hair was the color of a ripe chestnut. Sitting on the porch of an evening, that's what papa said.

YOUNG ANNA: But now ...

ANNA: But now ...

OLD ANNA: But now it's so white. Yes, I know!

YOUNG ANNA: Mama wouldn't recognize you.

OLD ANNA: Mama didn't live to be my age. She didn't have a gray hair on her head when she ... *(Lifts a strand of her hair and studies it)* But if I were to live alone in a small cottage ...

YOUNG ANNA: I could shave my head in the summer ...

OLD ANNA: And stain it with the juice of wild blackberries.

ANNA: What foolishness.

YOUNG ANNA: What fun!

ANNA: And in the winter?

YOUNG ANNA: In the winter my hair would be white.

OLD ANNA: As white as the hands of the Lord.

ANNA: What nonsense. You'll go home now and sign the agreement. Within a few weeks you'll be settled in your condominium.

YOUNG ANNA: Where you'll go to the beauty parlor, and chew each bite of food twenty times, and write down people's names so you won't forget. Boring!

ANNA: Practical.

YOUNG ANNA: If I were to live in a cottage I'd gather mushrooms in the rain ...

OLD ANNA: And fill my basket with wild grapes.

YOUNG ANNA: And I'd drink coffee before I comb my hair in the morning and never, never chew my food twenty times!

OLD ANNA: At sunset in December I would drink sherry from a crystal goblet while I listened to Mozart.

YOUNG ANNA: And on hot nights in July I'd drink beer straight from the can and sing bawdy songs!

OLD ANNA: And say naughty words out loud to see how they sound.

YOUNG ANNA: And I'd skate on the pond after dark ...

OLD ANNA: As I once did.

ANNA: You wouldn't dare. The ice might be thin.

YOUNG ANNA: What's the fun if you're afraid to skate on thin ice!

OLD ANNA: What's the fun?

ANNA: *(To YOUNG ANNA)* You're a silly old woman.

YOUNG ANNA: No!

OLD ANNA: *(Softly)* No.

ANNA: A faded rose doesn't refuse to drop it's petals!

YOUNG ANNA: But I do! I shall wrap my petals round me and skate on thin ice!

ANNA: Old animals are content to lie in the sun!

YOUNG ANNA: Phooey on lying in the sun!

OLD ANNA: *(Rubbing her temples)* Oh, dear, my head goes round and round. *(Rises, moves down stage and stands looking out over the water)* Why is it I can't seem to make a decision? Why can't I make up my mind?

(ANNA and YOUNG ANNA say swiftly and softly.)

ANNA: Condo.

YOUNG ANNA: Cottage.

ANNA: Golf.

YOUNG ANNA: Ants.

ANNA: Thin ice.

YOUNG ANNA: Phooey. Phooey. Phooey.

OLD ANNA: *(Closing her eyes, cries out)* My head is spinning round! *(Opens her eyes, looks out over the water, seems to see something at a distance)* Oh, my! *(Mimes taking glasses from her pocket and putting them on in order to see*

better. Takes off the glasses, rubs her eyes, replaces glasses)
Look!

ANNA & YOUNG ANNA: What? *(Simultaneously
moves to stand on either side of OLD ANNA)* Oh ... !

YOUNG ANNA: *(Softly)* Humpbacks!

OLD ANNA: *(Rubbing her eyes)* My eyes are all a-
dazzle ... Oh, aren't they wondrous! So ...

YOUNG ANNA: So ...

ANNA: So ...

OLD ANNA: So free.

YOUNG ANNA: Oh, look!

ANNA: That one is going to ...

YOUNG ANNA: To breach!

ALL THREE: Oooooooooh!

(Silence.)

OLD ANNA: They're on their way south.

ANNA: They'll be back.

OLD ANNA: How do they decide when to leave and
where to go? How do they know what to do?

YOUNG ANNA: They just know.

OLD ANNA: Yes. *(As she stands looking out over the
water a slow smile lights her face and she says softly)* Yes.
*(Shakes out her skirt, arranges her hair, retrieves the parasol
and says brightly)* I'd best get home and rest a bit before the
children arrive.

YOUNG ANNA: For the party!

OLD ANNA: My goodness, I suddenly feel ...

YOUNG ANNA & OLD ANNA: *(Twirling)* Quite gay!

OLD ANNA: And now I must hurry home. Little Dickie

Barlow is coming over to help me blow up the balloons. And if I've time to hide the presents we'll have a treasure hunt! Gracious, I'm feeling so fine I do believe I shall remember the name of everyone who comes through the door!

ANNA: *(Studies her)* It seems you've made a decision.

OLD ANNA: *(Surprised)* It seems I have.

ANNA: You're giving away the pickle fork?

OLD ANNA: It seems I am. *(Suddenly unsure)* Do you think Emma Gaul will like it?

ANNA: *(Exasperated)* Why wouldn't she? *(As OLD ANNA mimes the movements, ANNA raises the parasol)* Why wouldn't she? It's sterling.

(As YOUNG ANNA skips ahead, OLD ANNA laughs lightly. They exit.)

PROPERTY PLOT

There are no properties on stage when the play begins.

Properties brought on stage by a character:
> ... a parasol, flowered in shades of pink and rose, is carried on stage by OLD ANNA.

COSTUME PLOT

The three actresses are similarly dressed. All three wear skirts of a deep rose color. OLD ANNA wears a pink blouse. ANNA's and YOUNG ANNA's skirts are worn over pink leotards and tights.

The length of each skirt indicates the age of this woman at different stages of a long life. YOUNG ANNA's skirt falls just above the knee. ANNA's skirt is calf length, while the hem of OLD ANNA's skirt brushes the floor.

The costumes worn by the younger women are made of translucent material, helping establish these characters as voices of an inner dialogue. They wear pink ballet slippers.

VIVIEN
(COMIC DRAMA)

By PERCY GRANGER

2 men, 1 woman—Unit set

Recently staged to acclaim at Lincoln Center, this lovely piece is about a young stage director who visits his long-lost father in a nursing home and takes him to see a production of ''The Seagull'' that he staged. Along the way, each reveals a substantial truth about himself, and the journey eventually reaches its zenith in a restaurant after the performance. ''A revealing father-son portrait that gives additional certification to the author's position as a very original playwright.''—N.Y. Times. ''The dialogue has the accuracy of real people talking.''—N.Y. Post.

LANDSCAPE WITH WAITRESS
(COMEDY)

By ROBERT PINE

1 man, 1 woman—Interior

Arthur Granger is an unsuccessful novelist who lives a Walter Mitty-like fantasy existence. Tonight, he is dining out in an Italian restaurant which seems to have only one waitress and one customer—himself. As Arthur selects his dinner he has fantasies of romantic conquest, which he confides to the audience and to his notebook. While Arthur's fantasies take him into far-fetched plots, the waitress acts out the various characters in his fantasy. Soon, Arthur is chattering and dreaming away at such a quick clip that neither he nor we can be entirely sure of his sanity. Arthur finishes his dinner and goes home, ending as he began—as a lover *manqué*. '' . . . a landscape of the mind.''—Other Stages. '' . . . has moments of true originality and a bizarre sense of humor . . . a devious and slightly demented half-hour of comedy.''—N.Y. Times. Recently a hit at New York's excellent Ensemble Studio Theatre.

Other Publications for Your Interest

A GALWAY GIRL
(ALL GROUPS—DRAMA)

By GERALDINE ARON

1 man, 1 woman—Interior

A married couple, seated at opposite ends of a table, reminisce about their life together. Each presents the situation from his or her point of view, rarely addressing each other directly. The characters are young to begin with, then middle-aged, then old, then one of them dies. The anecdotes they relate are both humorous and tragic. Their lives seem wasted, yet at the end the wife's muted gesture of affection conveys the love that can endure through years of household bickering and incompatibility. A critical success in London, Ireland and the author's native South Africa. "A very remarkable play."—Times Literary Supplement, London. "A touching account of two wasted lives."—Daily Telegraph, London. "A minute tapestry cross-stitched with rich detail—invested with a strong strain of uncomfortable truths."—The Irish Times, Dublin.

TWO PART HARMONY
(PLAY)

By KATHARINE LONG

1 man, 1 woman—Interior

A play about a confrontation of wits between an alert, pre-adolescent girl and a mentally unsettled child-man. On a spring morning in 1959, eight year old Jessie Corington, home alone on a sick day from school, receives an unexpected visit from Hank Everett, a former friend of the family who used to look like Bobby Darin. From the moment he arrives, Hank's eccentric behavior challenges Jessie's cherished belief in adult maturity. Gradually, however, she welcomes her new found playmate and becomes entranced as he enlists her aid in a telephone search for his estranged wife. As the play builds, their bond of friendship is almost shattered when the violence beneath Hank's innocence surfaces against his will. "The work of an artist skilled in deft, understated draughtmanship."—Village Voice.